# PRIVIES AND WATER CLOSETS

## David J Eveleigh

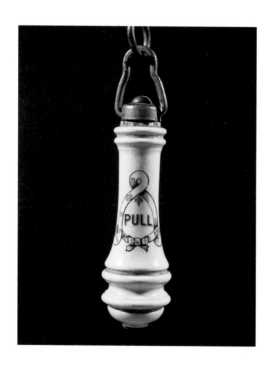

SHIRE PUBLICATIONS

First published in Great Britain in 2008 by Shire Publications Ltd, Midland House, West Way, Botley, Oxford OX2 0PH, United Kingdom.

443 Park Avenue South, New York, NY 10016, USA.

E-mail: shire@shirebooks.co.uk    www.shirebooks.co.uk

Shire Library no. 479    •    ISBN-13: 978 0 7478 0702 5

David J. Eveligh has asserted his right under the Copyright, Designs and Patents Act, 1988, to be identified as the author of this book.

Designed by Ken Vail Graphic Design, Cambridge, UK and typeset in Perpetua and Gill Sans. Printed in Malta by Gutenberg Press Ltd.

08 09 10 11 12    10 9 8 7 6 5 4 3 2 1

COVER IMAGE
*Milord Plumpudding avec Lady Arrhée,* Martinet, Paris, c.1814 (British Museum).

TITLE PAGE IMAGE
Ceramic cistern pull handle, 1887.

CONTENTS PAGE IMAGE
A view under the seat of a trough closet, 1900.

ACKNOWLEDGEMENTS
My thanks must go to Simon Kirby of Thomas Crapper & Co. Ltd and Terry Wooliscroft. They made valuable comments on the text and kindly gave me access to their archive Illustrations. I would also like to acknowledge the information I received from Felicity Harrison concerning the typhoid outbreak at Wakefield Prison caused by poorly maintained earth closets. Thanks are also due to the many other people who have taken the trouble to write to me with information and observations concerning the history of privies and water closets. However, the usual author's caveat applies: I alone take responsibility for any errors in the text.

Picture credits are as follows: Bristol Record Office, pages 9, 12 and 34; Bristol City Museum & Art Gallery, pages 6 and 33, British Museum, page 8 (top); Thomas Crapper & Co. Ltd., pages 4, 28, and 48 (top right); Duncan Marshall, page 23 (top); The National Portrait Gallery, page 18; Nottingham City Council, page 14; Geoffrey Pidgeon, page 55 (bottom left); Twyford Bathrooms, 42 (bottom), 46 (bottom), 47, 54, 56 (top left), 58 and 62 (top); The Worshipful Company of Clockmakers, page 29 (top).

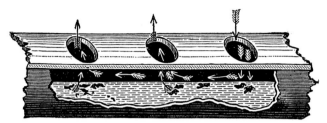

FIG. 206.—Water-closet Trough, bad arrangement.

# CONTENTS

# INTRODUCTION

TODAY, in the twenty-first century, we all know what a toilet is. We would not wish to be without one, we like them clean, and we generally prefer to use them in private. It is something we use rather than think about. We take toilets for granted and rarely pause to wonder how this essential domestic appliance came into being and who deserves the credit for its invention. The name 'Crapper' is frequently mentioned – but who was he? And can he justly be described as the inventor of the modern toilet?

As we begin to ponder the subject we encounter another difficulty: terminology. Toilet? An ugly word – an ugly thought – and so we skirt around the subject with euphemisms like 'loo' or 'cloakroom', while Americans talk of the 'rest room' or 'bathroom'. Take any dictionary published before about 1939 and a toilet is defined as 'a dressing table with a mirror', or the 'whole articles used in dressing'. So, what was the word for 'toilet' in 1898? 'Lavatory', perhaps? But apparently not: the same dictionary defines a 'lavatory' as 'a place for washing', even though by then many towns and cities had provided public lavatories, where, of course, it was possible to do more than wash hands.

Technically speaking, the correct term for the modern toilet is 'water closet' and the association of the word 'closet' for what we are concerned with here dates back many centuries. Water closet is often abbreviated to 'WC' and used this way by architects, surveyors and even the French, who have embraced this Anglo-Saxon acronym and made it their own. Interestingly this is not the first time that the French have looked to the English to find a name for their toilets. In aristocratic circles in early eighteenth-century France, a closet provided with a flush was apparently termed 'lieu à l'anglaise,' as the device was understood to have been imported from England. Then, strangely, this term returned to England, abbreviated simply to lieu and over time anglicised to 'loo'. Another old word for toilet was 'privy'. In *The Chambers Dictionary* of 1898 this is defined as a 'necessary house', something which was unavoidable and indispensable. Like 'closet', the word 'privy' is centuries old and conveniently it takes us back in time to the beginning of this brief history...

Opposite:
The showrooms of
Thomas Crapper &
Co. in the King's
Road, Chelsea,
c.1908.

# PRIVY-MIDDENS

FOR centuries, sanitary arrangements within homes at all social levels were often portable and involved a degree of improvisation. In the seventeenth and eighteenth centuries, small rooms or 'closets' were often found adjoining upstairs bed chambers where 'calls of nature' could be answered comfortably and in some privacy sitting on a commode or close stool containing a pan under the seat. A grotesque French satirical print of c.1814 entitled *Milord Plumpudding avec Lady Arrhée*, shows a fat, fleshy, varicose-veined Englishman sitting in his night shift on a high backed commode beside a canopied bed. In aristocratic circles, close stools could be sumptuous, like those recorded in the will of Arabella Stewart (1575–1615) of Hardwick Hall in 1601. There were several covered in leather but the one in her own bed chamber was covered in blue cloth and fringed with red and black silk. For the well-to-do, the emptying of the pan was a servant's responsibility but it could be messy if there was an accident, like the one an amused Samuel Pepys (1633–1703) recorded in May 1663. 'I up… and hear that my wife and her maid Ashwell had between them spilt the pot of piss and turd upon the floor and stool and God knows what, and were mighty merry washing of it clean.'

Chamber pots were also used around the house. They were once common in bedrooms, placed under the bed – the author can recall this arrangement as an infant staying at his grandmother's house at Inghead Terrace, Shelf, near Halifax in the late 1950s. Almost three hundred years earlier, in September 1665, Samuel Pepys found himself 'mightely troubled with a looseness' and finding no chamber pot was forced 'to rise and shit in the chimney' – twice. In 1784, a Frenchman, François de la Rochfoucauld (1765–1848), staying in Suffolk, recorded with disgust the English country house practice of urinating into chamber pots in full view of the dining table. Another French satirical print of c.1814 shows this scene – *L'Après Dîner* – but suggests that the aim of a drunken English gentleman was none too straight.

The fixed sanitary arrangement was the privy. It went by several other names including the 'necessary house', the 'house of office' and, in eighteenth-century London at least, the 'bog house'. Whatever the name, the privy

Opposite:
Ramshackle timber privies overhanging the River Frome at St James's Back in the centre of Bristol by Henry O'Neil, c.1821.

Chamber pots –
and their misuse –
are in full view of
the dining table in
this French print
of 1814, *L'Après
Dîner des Anglais.*

was very different from the modern toilet in having no water supply and no drain. It consisted of a fixed wooden seat containing a round or slightly oval hole placed over a void (the midden or cesspit) in which the human dung simply piled up. In larger dwellings, privies were occasionally found incorporated within the main structure, housed in projecting garderobe turrets as at Little Moreton Hall in Cheshire and (at the level of the yeoman farmer) at Ostridge Manor Farm, a substantial sixteenth-century stone farmhouse at Pilning, South Gloucestershire. Privies were also commonly attached to the furthest end of the ground-floor service wing and reached by a separate external door. Some were even located in cellars. In 1847, Henry Austin, an engineer and Secretary to the Health of Towns Association, was appalled to find houses in the High Street of Worcester where the 'necessaries' were placed in the cellars, 'from which offensive effluvium', he wrote, 'is perpetually poisoning the atmosphere in the houses'. Pepys also seems to have been familiar with cellar privies. On 8 July 1663, he wrote in his diary, 'and then down into the cellar and up and down with Mr Turner [his neighbour] to see where his vault for turds may be made bigger, or another made [by] him, which I think may well be.'

In large houses
servants emptied
the slops from
chamber pots into
covered pails. This
one of 1904 is
made of galvanised
iron.

Many privies were separate altogether from the house and located some distance away, often at the far end of the garden. They were typically small structures that followed the vernacular building traditions of the locality. Roofs were variously single- or double-pitched and doors provided with a 'saw-tooth' top to provide ventilation; some had a small window. In the countryside, a privy of crumbling stone with a

In *Night*, William Hogarth shows a chamber pot being emptied through a window on to the people in the street below, 1738.

Below:
Plans of town houses on the Quay in Bristol showing the necessary houses in the back courts, *c*.1720.

double-pitched roof covered with an old rambling rose, jasmine or honeysuckle could present quite a pretty sight, tucked away in a bottom corner of the garden.

Inside, the fixed wooden seat – generally of scrubbed deal – usually occupied the full width of the rear wall whilst a simple panelling of deal planks often extended 2 or 3 feet above the seat. Privies were not always as private as the name might suggest: many surviving privy seats have two holes although examples with three, four or even six holes have been recorded. The holes were often graded in size with a small one, sometimes set lower, for infants and small children. Separate lift-off lids of wood with turned wooden handles covered the holes and the ghastly sight and smell of the human dung piled up in the pit or void beneath the seat.

After more than a hundred years of flushing WCs, it is difficult for most of us to comprehend the awful reality of the ordinary privy. In the late 1890s, Percy

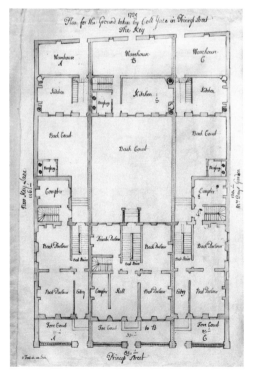

Above: A timber privy with a one-hole seat slowly decaying in the overgrown garden of a cottage near Congresbury, North Somerset, photographed in 1996.

Top right:
Three-seat privy with hinged lids.

Above right: Corner of a 10-foot-wide three-seat privy at Elm Tree Farm, Hallatrow, North Somerset. A lift-off elm lid covers a 7-inch hole.

Boulnois, City Engineer for Liverpool, called them 'abominations'. A few were placed over a stream so the waste was immediately washed away by the flow of water, but these were the exception. In the average privy, the accumulation of raw sewage was never far from the privy seat. In working-class town houses built in the mid nineteenth century it was common for two or more privies to be connected by a short inclined drain to a common cesspool. In 1842 in the newly established railway town of Swindon, imposing 'Jacobethan' style cottages were built in Bristol Street for the growing industrial workforce. They had back yards that were 21 feet long and at the back of each was a dust hole for the disposal of household refuse and a privy. Neighbouring privies were placed side by side in the yards and each pair drained into a cesspool located under the 8-foot-wide alleyway that ran between two parallel rows of cottages. The cesspools were connected by a 12-inch diameter drain running the length of the alley, and access to each was through a separate manhole.

But many ordinary privies were positioned directly over the pit or midden. The London bog hole, according to Henry Mayhew (1812–87), writing in 1850, was lined in brickwork or masonry; it was relatively shallow, containing about a cubic yard of sewage although some were deeper. It was also common for cesspools to be left unlined, or for any brickwork to be only partially fixed with mortar, so that the liquid portion of the sewage could seep away, thus reducing the bulk of the waste and delaying the inevitable emptying. As a result there were many instances of raw sewage seeping into nearby wells, contaminating local supplies of drinking water and spreading diseases such as diarrhoea, typhoid and cholera. In 1848 in Bethnal Green, on the eastern edge of London, Hector Gavin, a doctor and member of the Committee of the Health of Towns Association, found poorly built small houses with wooden privies erected over holes provided with a 'surface hollow' so the fluid could drain away. This liquid soil, oozing from the privies and cesspools, he noted, was often concealed by dust and cinders piled up in the alleys and yards of the houses. In many instances, the sewage had actually penetrated the walls of houses and even saturated the floors, rendering them 'very quagmires of filth'. He also found some rows of houses where the privies drained into filthy, black ditches filled with 'semi-fluid foetid pestilential matter'. Many of the privies he came across were 'most dilapidated' and as a result dangerous to use: one woman, he reported, had even fallen through a rotten privy floor and drowned in the filth beneath.

In the overcrowded slums of rapidly expanding early Victorian towns and cities the privy was usually the only sanitary device available. Hector Gavin reckoned that in Bethnal Green there were not fifty WCs for the 82,000 inhabitants of this large parish, and that the provision of privies was often wholly inadequate; it was common for just one to be shared by several households. In Sunderland in the 1840s it was calculated that there was only one privy for every seventy-six persons. Shared privies were often the very worst, suffering heavy usage but rarely cleaned or emptied. In Worcester, Henry Austin came across one that was used by more than fifteen families; it was, he wrote, 'one of the most horrible examples of loathsomeness and indecency' he had ever seen. In Bethnal Green, Hector Gavin visited Martha Court off Martha Street, which contained thirteen two-roomed houses which shared three privies in 'an offensive state' whilst, in Turville Buildings, one 'nasty and horribly offensive' privy was shared by seven houses. In the 'excessively dirty and foul' environment of Shepherd's Court he found confined privies with excrement 'scattered abroad'.

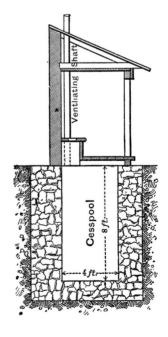

A privy-midden located over an 8-foot-deep cesspool, c.1895

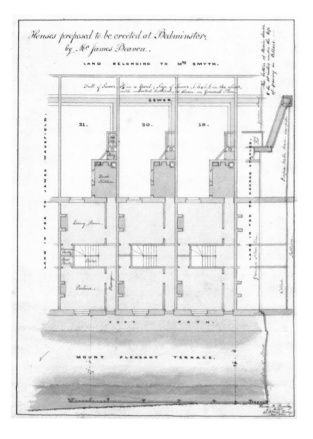

Plans of terraced houses in Mount Pleasant, Bedminster, Bristol, built in 1851. Each house has a privy in the back yard, which drains into a sewer running across the back of the row.

Everywhere he came across stagnant pools of night soil, slimy mud, decomposing garbage and dung heaps giving off the most disgusting odour.

Just a decade earlier, Charles Dickens (1812–70) had conveyed a similar picture of Jacob's Island in Bermondsey on the south bank of the Thames. 'Every repulsive lineament of poverty, every loathsome indication of filth, rot and garbage' was to be encountered in this island bounded by a muddy inlet of the River Thames – the Folly Ditch. It was here that Bill Sykes met his end attempting to escape from a vengeful crowd in *Oliver Twist*. According to Dickens, houses built on a wooden bridge over the ditch at Mill Lane had 'crazy wooden galleries common to the backs of half a dozen houses with holes from which to look upon the slime beneath'. These were privies that decanted the human excreta straight into the muddy waters. Similar privies overhung the River Frome as it wound its sluggish course through the centre of Bristol. Dr William Budd (1811–80), a local doctor, described the scene in 1844. The privies were situated in galleries projecting from the backs of old houses – slum properties – lining the river. The galleries overhung a bank of mud that was swept away only at spring tide; between high tides, he observed, the state of things was 'too loathsome and disgusting to describe'. Of course, for the Victorian sanitary reformer there was a moral dimension to the issue. As William Budd stated, 'people living among [such conditions] necessarily become coarse, filthy and brutalised.'

The type of privy overhanging a river did, however, possess two advantages over its ordinary counterpart. It was inconceivable that it could ever overflow – Biblical floods excepted – and it did not require emptying. For the ordinary privy with its cesspool, pit or shallow void, the occasional cleaning out was an unavoidable, horrible event. The smell was unbearable, as the London journalist Henry Mayhew discovered in 1850 when he went to see one being emptied. The stench, he reported, was 'literally sickening'. As a result it was usually carried out during the hours of darkness by nightmen. In July 1663, Samuel Pepys gave some idea of the disruption caused by this nocturnal activity. 'This night, Mr Turner's house [of office] being to be emptied out of my cellar and therefore I think to sit up a little longer than ordinary ... and so to bed, leaving the men below in the cellar emptying the turds up through Mr Turner's own house.'

In poor districts, privies were often left until they overflowed. In Bethnal Green, Hector Gavin entered a house in Pleasant Row, where 'the privy was close by and full and overflowing, covering the yard with its putrescent filth ...' In Swindon in the 1840s, the new railway cottages suffered

Nightmen emptying a cesspit by lantern light from Mayhew's *London Labour and the London Poor*, 1861.

serious overcrowding and outbreaks of disease were commonplace: in 1849, there were serious outbreaks of smallpox, typhus and cholera. The principal cause of disease was the stagnant, polluted water overflowing from blocked cesspools. The surface drainage of the unpaved back yards, courts and alleys containing the privies and cesspools had insufficient dip to carry the surface water to the deep drains. The emptying of cesspools was sometimes neglected owing to the sheer offensiveness of the operation. The cost was another deterrent, especially for the poor: in the 1840s, the usual rate for emptying a cesspool in London was a shilling when lower-class rents ranged from one to five shillings a week. This was clearly beyond the means of many poor families although the maintenance of the privies was usually a landlord's responsibility. But landlords were also inclined to postpone the work, sometimes delaying until it was too late (until after fever had broken out) and then acting only to prevent their property acquiring a bad name and becoming untenable.

# DRY PRIVIES

IT IS CLEAR from the accounts left by Austin, Gavin and others that a sanitary form of anarchy and total chaos existed in most large British towns and cities in the mid nineteenth century. A 'Report on the Sanitary Condition of the Labouring Population of Great Britain' by Sir Edwin Chadwick (1800–90) in 1842 and a Health of Towns Commission report carried out in 1844–45 confirmed the widespread nature of the problem. Only a privileged minority had access to water closets: in Birmingham in the early 1860s, they were found in just 5 per cent of houses. The situation in most towns had been exacerbated by the massive population increases of the previous half century. By the 1850s, sanitary arrangements which might have been acceptable before 1800 had become intolerable and the cause of epidemics of diseases such as cholera and typhoid. The first Public Health Act of 1848 provided local urban authorities with the power to become local boards of health in order to create some sort of 'sanitary order'. They were also given powers to levy a general district rate to raise the necessary funds to carry out improvements.

So, the wider adoption of the WC at all social levels might have appeared the obvious solution. But water closets brought their own problems even if the householder was spared some of the worst aspects of the ordinary privy. Their use had been gradually increasing from the late eighteenth century and by the 1820s and 1830s they were found in many middle-class homes. In 1844, Thomas Cubitt (1788–1855), the London builder, estimated that in the previous twenty years the use of WCs in London had increased tenfold. Some were complicated and expensive but the more fundamental problem was that a water closet was only effective when it was connected to a mains system of water and drainage, a circuit that came to be known as the 'water carriage system'. To work efficiently, a water closet required generous quantities of water to provide a powerful flush to eject the waste and then connections to a sewerage system to carry the effluent harmlessly away. A WC operating outside the 'water carriage system' was little better than a privy.

The simple fact was that by the second quarter of the nineteenth century water closet technology – and its adoption – had run ahead of sewerage

Opposite:
Privy building at Littlewood Place off Windmill Lane in Sneinton, an industrial suburb of south-east Nottingham which grew rapidly in the second half of the nineteenth century, 1 July 1912.

Left: In this drawing of 1883, a WC is shown draining into a cesspool that is overflowing and contaminating the basement kitchen.

Below left: Until the late 1800s, the poor generally relied on public water supplies like this street pump. Consequently they were particularly vulnerable to water-borne diseases such as cholera and typhoid carried in contaminated water. *Fun*, 1866.

Below right: In early Victorian London, sewer hunters made a living retrieving valuables such as coins, silver utensils and jewellery accidentally flushed down the WC. From Mayhew's *London Labour and the London Poor*, 1861.

FUN.—August 18, 1866.

DEATH'S DISPENSARY.

OPEN TO THE POOR, GRATIS, BY PERMISSION OF THE PARISH.

THE SEWER-HUNTER.

technology and provision. In 1851, Mayhew reckoned that about 50 per cent of London's houses lacked drainage to sewers; in other towns the figure was probably higher. The majority of WCs drained into cesspools in back yards, perpetuating one of the greatest evils of the privy-midden: that liquid raw sewage could contaminate local supplies of drinking water. Indeed, due to the large volume of water used by a WC, a cesspool connected to a WC was more likely to overflow than when used with an ordinary privy. As Chadwick highlighted in his 1842 report, insanitary conditions bred disease. In Bristol, during the cholera epidemic of 1849 that killed 444 people in the city, several well-to-do people died in Richmond Terrace, an imposing row of large houses in fashionable Clifton. The cause was ultimately traced to contamination of the nearby Richmond Spring by seepage from the cesspools behind the houses.

Edwin Chadwick
(1800–90)

Other water closets were connected to existing street sewers, which usually drained into the nearest river. Such was the case in London, where,

Death in the water of the Thames as seen by *Punch*, 10 July 1858, during London's 'Great Stink' of that summer.

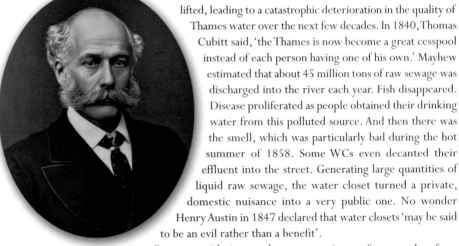

Sir Joseph
Bazalgette
(1819–91)

from 1815, restrictions on connections to the sewers were lifted, leading to a catastrophic deterioration in the quality of Thames water over the next few decades. In 1840, Thomas Cubitt said, 'the Thames is now become a great cesspool instead of each person having one of his own.' Mayhew estimated that about 45 million tons of raw sewage was discharged into the river each year. Fish disappeared. Disease proliferated as people obtained their drinking water from this polluted source. And then there was the smell, which was particularly bad during the hot summer of 1858. Some WCs even decanted their effluent into the street. Generating large quantities of liquid raw sewage, the water closet turned a private, domestic nuisance into a very public one. No wonder Henry Austin in 1847 declared that water closets 'may be said to be an evil rather than a benefit'.

For some mid-nineteenth-century sanitary reformers, therefore, the water closet was far from the obvious solution. At the time, some towns would have nothing to do with them, like Manchester, where in 1862 the Town Clerk, speaking to a Parliamentary Select Committee, referred to water closets as 'troublesome devices'. Nevertheless, some towns and cities opted for the water carriage system early on. Sir Joseph Bazalgette (1819–91) pioneered the use of a system of intercepting sewers when, as Chief Engineer of the Metropolitan Board of Works (established in 1856), he oversaw the construction of some 1,300 miles of sewers and 82 miles of main intercepting sewers across London. The system carried the sewage to large settlement reservoirs at Beckton on the north bank of the Thames and Crossness on the south and from these it was discharged into the Thames. Other towns and cities followed, including Liverpool, Bristol, Portsmouth and Reading. Bazalgette's advice was frequently sought and between 1858 and 1875 he produced thirty-two reports as consultant. Bristol was one city that called on his expertise. In the 1840s, it had the third highest mortality rate in the country, being surpassed only by Liverpool and Manchester. In 1851, however, Bristol adopted the 1848 Public Health Act and established a Local Board of Health which by 1866 had laid over 100 miles of mains sewers under the city's streets and enforced connections to the system. But the capital outlay of such schemes was considerable. Bazalgette's scheme in London cost over £4 million and there were those for whom this scale of expenditure was a major argument against expanding the use of water closets.

But there were other objections. The water carriage system was also heavily criticised in some quarters for wasting a valuable source of manure. Bitterly criticising the discharge of raw sewage into the River Thames, Henry

Mayhew wryly observed in 1851, 'we import guano and drink a solution of our own faeces'. Some towns that had invested in sewerage systems – like Reading and Leamington Spa – attempted to harness the value of liquid sewage by using it to irrigate specially designed farms. But in most cases, the modest income that the liquid sewage (heavily diluted with water) yielded as farm manure scarcely covered the substantial costs involved in conveying it to the land. Some reformers strongly believed the alternative solution was to keep the human waste dry and cover it with a dry substance such as earth or ash so that the excrement was immediately deodorised and then broken down to create a rich manure. The debate between supporters of the water carriage system and those who argued for the dry conservancy method raged for over twenty-five years. It was to lead to the invention of an entirely new and different type of closet, the 'EC', using earth rather than water, and also to a plethora of improved 'dry' privies in many towns particularly in the Midlands and the north of England.

Moule's earth closet with pull-up apparatus, 1889.

One of the most effective supporters of the dry system, and a robust opponent of the water system, was the Reverend Henry Moule (1801–80), vicar of Fordington near Dorchester, Dorset. Following experiments carried out using his own household, he took out a patent in 1860 for an earth closet that relied on the ability of surface garden soil, naturally rich in bacteria, to break down human faeces rapidly and completely. Moule discovered that if the earth and excrement were carefully mixed together and then kept dry in a rough open shed, the soil quickly recovered its absorbent powers. He calculated that a single cartload of soil would serve two or three people for up to twelve months.

Moule devised several different designs and by the mid 1860s they were being manufactured under patent protection by Moule's Patent Earth Closet Company in London. There were other makers, including Moser of Southampton and John Parker of Woodstock, who in 1873 claimed his closets 'keep the place perfectly sweet and wholesome'. The most familiar and longest-lived type was the self-contained portable wooden unit – like an ordinary commode – with a round hole in the seat. A strong, wide-rimmed bucket of galvanised or enamelled iron was placed under the seat; this could be removed for emptying through a door at the front. The back-rest of the closet contained a hopper filled with soil, and every time the closet was used a small portion was released to cover the fresh faeces. In 1873, George

An earth closet
used in a cottage at
Coalpit Heath,
South
Gloucestershire,
until the late 1950s.

Wilson, Medical Officer of Health for mid-Warwickshire, reckoned that 1½ pounds of soil was required to deodorise each stool, including the urine. Earth closets were either operated manually by pulling a short brass handle at the base of the hopper or were self-acting. These semi-automatic closets contained a strong spring under the seat, which connected with the earth supply so that the very act of rising from the closet ensured a quantity of soil fell into the bucket. They were intended for 'careless users' – a much-loved term of Victorian sanitarians that generally included anyone residing in an institution and nearly everyone who was poor.

Extravagant claims were made by the 'dry school' as to the value of sewage as rich agricultural manure. Carefully harnessed, they said, it could be turned to cash so that the dry system could run at a profit instead of being, like the water carriage system, a drain on local rates. Moule's earth closet was a vital component of his case against the water system. He argued that his closets were cheaper than water closets, simpler to use and more robust. In 1863 he claimed that in a 'borough' town, which had adopted the water carriage system, a national school had spent £70 connecting water closets to the sewers but could have purchased his self-acting closets for less than £20. From the 1860s the earth closet received considerable support from other public health reformers, including Medical Officers of Health such as George Wilson and the engineer, J. Bailey Denton. But their endorsements were not without caveats. The successful operation of earth closets depended upon a plentiful supply of soil, but also on careful management. It was important that urine was not added to the bucket. Everything had to be kept dry. The earth closet, therefore, worked best in managed communities, such as estate villages and various institutions, including schools, workhouses and prisons.

In the mid 1870s, the Rothschild estate at Halton, Buckinghamshire, provided an excellent example of 'best practice' in earth closet management. One man – a 'scavenger' – was employed to take a cartload of dried earth around the estate filling the hoppers of the 170 to 180 closets in use and even, if necessary, levelling the soil in the vaults under the seat. The used earth was taken to an open shed where it was dried over a large iron plate heated from below. Providing the closets were kept dry, there was no smell although it was noted that where the vault was not watertight they were little better than common privies. A similar picture emerges from Wakefield Prison, where they had been introduced in 1866. By 1870 there were 776 in use and, superficially, the scheme appeared to work well. Prisoners were employed to empty the closets and, using the manure, excellent vegetables were grown within the prison walls. But during the winter of 1874–75, the prison experienced a serious outbreak of typhoid, killing eighteen inmates. The ensuing investigation established that some of the closets were found 'most disgustingly dirty through misuse and neglect'. Some of the emptied pails were returned to the closets with faecal matter stuck to the sides. Mis-management of the earth closets was clearly a contributory factor in the spread of the disease amongst the inmates.

The chief weakness of the earth closet system, however, was the difficulty of obtaining sufficient supplies of earth and providing the means of drying and storing it. At Halton the system required 200 tons of earth annually. What might have been feasible on a well-ordered country estate was virtually impossible to realise in a large, crowded industrial town. By the late 1860s, it was apparent that the application of the earth closet was bound to be limited and largely restricted to rural areas. In the countryside, where fresh loamy earth was to be found everywhere but water was often in short supply, the earth closet represented a major improvement on the old common privy. Indeed, the earth closet enjoyed a long and successful life in many rural districts and some remained in use until the 1950s and 1960s.

Various dry systems of excreta removal were, nevertheless, widely adopted in northern manufacturing towns in the third quarter of the nineteenth century. Many local authorities initiated their own forms of improved privies, many of which relied on ash in place of earth as the deodorising agent. The great advantage of ash, of course, was that virtually every Victorian urban household generated its own supply through the use of coal fires for heating and cooking. It cost nothing – it was already on site –

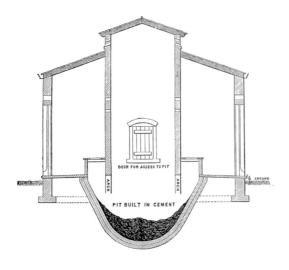

A Nottingham ash closet of the 1870s. The pit was nearly 5 feet deep and emptied once every three months. Ash thrown in through the middle door did not always cover the 'dejections' in the centre of the midden, causing a 'considerable stench'.

and there were some who argued that the deodorising and absorbent powers of ash were equal to earth. Other deodorising agents were tried, including soot, charcoal and various industrial waste products such as coal tar, used bark from tanneries and soap boilers' waste, but none of these could compete with domestic ash: dry, odourless and absolutely free.

The design of improved ash privies generally incorporated two principles: the pit was made waterproof to prevent the liquid portion of the sewage seeping into nearby wells and springs; and most were made smaller to prevent 'undue accumulation', as George Wilson explained in 1873. The pit of a Nottingham ash privy, for example, was made of brickwork in cement to make it impervious. It was 4 feet 10 inches deep and curved in towards the base so that the waste would gravitate towards the centre of the pit. The privy structure contained an opening 2 feet above the ground, through which ashes could be thrown over the contents of the pit. In Manchester, the pits were lined with Rochdale flags set in mortar and some at least were made with a bevel to the base to facilitate the emptying. The pit was also shallow, being no more than 3 feet deep. In 1864, Mr Wallworth, of the Manchester Scavengers' Department,

A Manchester pail closet with cinder sifter, c.1895.

said, 'I believe that no known or projected system yet has been found to answer the requirements of a large or small town equal to the Lancashire ash pit.' The Burnley ash midden was built over a pit of glazed stoneware and was considerably smaller so that its contents could be easily removed. Similar receptacles were used in Staffordshire and one from a house at Coalpit Hill near Newcastle-under-Lyme was last emptied in March 1980, just in time to be recovered by the Gladstone Pottery Museum at Longton, Stoke-on-Trent.

Privies at the rear of a Victorian brick terrace, Albion Street, Chester.

Gradually the ash pit closet was replaced in many northern towns by the pail or tub closet. This was a great improvement on those with a vault as the small size of the container necessitated frequent removal of the waste. Manchester was one of the first cities to make the transition from privies to pail closets. Ash was still used to deodorise the faeces but it was first thrown on to a cinder sifter consisting of a wire riddle or sieve placed at a height of about 4 feet behind the closet. The fine ash passed through the sieve to a chute above a round iron pail while the larger cinders rolled off to a store at the back where they could be removed and re-used as fuel. Self-acting mechanical cinder sifters manufactured by Morrell's Sanitary Appliance Company (first patented in 1866) were in use in Manchester and Salford by 1872. As J. Bailey Denton wryly explained in a lecture given at the School of Military Engineering at Chatham in 1876, 'the movement of the sifter is effected automatically when the closet is used, or rather the user of the closet effects the object without knowing it.'

By the mid 1870s, the pail system was in operation in many other Midland and northern towns. Rochdale adopted it in about 1868 and ten years later had 7,504 pails in use, although that still left 1,200 privy-middens remaining.

A Rochdale horse-
drawn night soil
van with two pails
on view, c.1895.

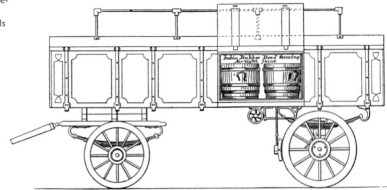

Regular collection of the tubs was vital to the successful operation of the pail system and in Rochdale four-wheeled, horse-drawn night soil vans went around the town collecting the filled pails with a sealed lid and supplying disinfected replacements. The town was divided into six districts and each tub was numbered so the collections could be carefully monitored. The contents of the pails were taken to a municipal depot, where a commendable level of recycling took place. Cinders and broken pottery were ground up for mortar while rags, glass and iron were sold. The excrement was emptied into a trench and eventually sold as manure. The result was that Rochdale became a healthier place to live in: between 1870 and 1878, the death rate apparently dropped from twenty-seven to twenty-one per hundred. A similar scheme operated in Salford where 1,000 pails were in use by the mid 1870s. Manure works were established by the corporation and, for a short while at least,

Pail closet at
Tytherington,
Gloucestershire,
built between 1902
and 1906 and
photographed
shortly before
demolition in
2000.

24

made a profit of nearly £1,500 a year through selling the manure and recycling the cinders and other materials.

In some towns the pails were supplied with a lining of ash or some other absorbent material to absorb the liquid. The Goux absorbent pail, patented in 1868, was lined with a mixture of ash, dry street sweepings, factory waste and calcium sulphate which was pressed down with a mould. The system was adopted in Halifax, where by the mid 1870s 3,000 of Goux's tubs were in use. Providing the pails were thoroughly prepared, urine would be absorbed by the lining, leaving the excreta reasonably dry. If they were emptied regularly they represented a major improvement on the former midden system. But there was still an element of unpleasantness in their use and it was also discovered that the packing material tended to generate swarms of 'minute flies'!

In Halifax, use of the Goux system continued to expand into the 1880s but by then the dry conservancy movement was quickly running short of momentum. In 1875, a committee was appointed by the recently established Local Government Board to assess the various methods of sewage disposal. It concluded, 'the retention … of refuse and excreta … in cesspools … or other places in the midst of towns, must be utterly condemned and none of the (so-called) dry-earth or pail systems or improved privies can be approved other than as palliatives for cesspit middens.' The following year, a committee of the Society of Arts investigating the health of towns concluded that 'for use within the house no system has been found in practice to take the place of the water closet'. And delivering a final 'nail in the coffin' to the dry conservancy argument, the report affirmed that ash reduced the value of the excreta as manure and that no dry system repaid the cost of collection. The fundamental flaw with all dry closets was that they stored excrement instead of quickly disposing of it, so they invariably stank. They were clearly unsuited, therefore, to being part of any well-appointed house and, like the old privy, were of necessity located in an outbuilding. Consequently, the Victorian middle classes would have nothing to do with them: the future lay, after all, with the water closet.

Below left:
Pierre Goux's excrement pail with absorbent lining.

Below right:
A late development of the dry closet was introduced by E. L. Jackson in 1924. This was the 'Elsan' chemical toilet, which used formaldehyde to neutralise the waste.

# EARLY WATER CLOSET TECHNOLOGY

T YPHOID was no respecter of persons. It targeted not only the poor and prison convicts as at Wakefield but killed Prince Albert in 1861 and then in 1871 nearly carried off his son and heir, 'Bertie', the Prince of Wales. In November 1871 he contracted the disease at Sandringham, Norfolk, and for several weeks the country waited with bated breath for the latest news bulletin by electric telegraph as he lay critically ill. Slowly he recovered and, while he convalesced, his illness was attributed to faulty drains at the royal residence. Upon learning this, the prince – according to *Harper's Monthly Magazine* – famously exclaimed, 'If I were not a prince, I would be a plumber.' It was in this decade that sanitary science finally came of age and began to respond to the public health crisis that had first emerged so graphically in Edwin Chadwick's reports some thirty years earlier. The fatal connection between water supplies and endemic diseases such as cholera and typhoid was finally becoming clear following the pioneering work of Dr John Snow (1813–58) and William Budd in Bristol. Plumbing was at last being transformed from an ancient art and craft into a modern science allied to a new type of professional, the sanitary engineer.

Sanitary engineers came from a variety of backgrounds. Some were civil engineers, like J. Bailey Denton, an expert in land drainage. William Eassie (1832–88), who wrote and lectured on sanitary equipment in the 1870s, had served as assistant engineer at the Renkioi Hospital during the Crimean War whilst Percy Boulnois had worked under Bazalgette for the Metropolitan Board of Works. Others were manufacturers. Henry Doulton (1820–97) came to prominence as an ally of the water carriage 'camp' through establishing new works for the manufacture of impervious salt-glazed drain pipes at Lambeth in 1845. By 1854 it was estimated that his company was producing a fifth of all sewer pipes in the country. He went on to become a leading maker of ceramic sanitary ware. In 1887, he was knighted by Queen Victoria. Along with two other well-known Victorian manufacturers, Twyford

Opposite:
The 'Optimus' valve closet by Dent & Hellyer, c.1880, in a typical wooden enclosure in Sir John Soane's House, 12 and 13 Lincoln's Inn Fields, London.

and Shanks, Doulton remains a household name today for sanitary ware (although the name 'Doulton' ceased to be used for bathroom appliances in 2006). Other important names – George Jennings and Edmund Sharpe, to name just two – have sadly fallen away, but one name towers over all in the popular mind and that name is, of course, Thomas Crapper.

It is quite extraordinary how his name continues to be associated with the invention of the water closet. The line of thought seems to go something like this: Thomas Crapper had the right name for the job (the verb to 'crap' predates the man), he was a Victorian and the Victorians were invariably innovative and inventive; therefore, he *must* have invented the WC. Thomas Crapper may be legendary, but he had a very real existence. He was born in 1836 near Doncaster, Yorkshire, and having travelled to London at an early age and worked for a plumber, he established his own business in 1861. In 1866 he moved to Marlborough Road, off the King's Road in Chelsea, where he established a reputation for sanitary ware of the highest quality. Crapper was invited to supply plumbing and fittings at Sandringham; the company subsequently held a further three royal warrants.

After his death in 1910, the business continued to trade independently until 1966 when it was taken over by a rival firm, John Bolding & Co., but they went bankrupt in 1969. That might have been the end of the story. The company no longer traded but the firm survived in limbo, registered at Companies House. In 1999, it was acquired by Simon Kirby, who at the time was running his own architectural salvage company. Since then Simon Kirby has breathed new life into a venerable sanitary firm, producing a range of bathroom fittings that combine modern materials and current manufacturing standards with the original late-Victorian designs. The toilet basin is incidentally called the 'Venerable'. However, I know he would agree that the original Thomas Crapper cannot be credited with the invention of the water closet, even though he took out several patents for sanitary equipment (the first, in 1863, being for a self-rising closet seat, presumably for those simple folk who could not grasp the essentials of using a WC properly). In fact, the introduction of the water closet cannot even be credited to the Victorians, since the first patent for a water closet was

Thomas Crapper (1836–1910).

The 'Venerable' closet from the current range of sanitaryware by Thomas Crapper & Co. Ltd.

actually taken out in 1775 by Alexander Cummings (*c.*1732–1814), a leading London horologist. Significantly, Cummings did not claim the water closet as his invention, merely seeking patent protection for a 'water closet upon a new construction'.

The documented history of the water closet stretches back nearly two centuries before 1775. In 1592, Sir John Harington (1561–1612), a godson of Queen Elizabeth I, installed a closet of his own design at his house at Kelston near Bath in readiness for a visit by his godmother. We know about this because he wrote about it in a rather silly book, *A New Discourse on a Stale Subject: Called the Metamorphosis of Ajax*, published in 1596. Ajax was a pun on 'jakes', common slang for 'privy' at the time.

References to water closets in the seventeenth century are scarce but they appear more frequently after 1700. Water closets, it would seem – at least in high quality houses – were known throughout the eighteenth century. John Wood the Elder (1704–54) installed them in a house for the Duke of Chandos in Bath in 1728, whilst Lord Chesterfield (1694–1773) had one on the first floor of his house in Grosvenor Square in 1733. (It was Lord Chesterfield, incidentally, who advised his son to tear pages from books of poetry for use as toilet paper.) After 1750, the use of water closets seems to have increased. In about 1879, Samuel Stephens Hellyer, a leading London plumber and sanitary engineer, found two closets in Osterley House in west London, which he reckoned may have been installed when

Alexander
Cummings
(*c.*1732–1814).

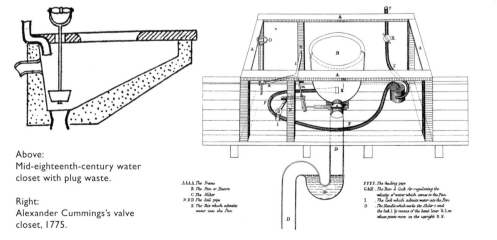

Above:
Mid-eighteenth-century water closet with plug waste.

Right:
Alexander Cummings's valve closet, 1775.

the house was first built by brothers Robert and John Adam in 1761. These closets had marble pans that were emptied by lifting a plug attached to a vertical rod. Flush water was delivered from a service pipe connecting to an overhead cistern.

In his patent of 1775, Cummings introduced a mechanically operated sliding valve – he called it the 'slider' – which, when closed, held a generous reserve of clean water in the WC basin; this effectively drowned solids and also served as a seal against sewer gas in the soil pipe. Pulling on a handle recessed in the seat caused the valve to slide to one side and the waste to disappear. By a simple lever connection, the inlet valve admitting the flush water from an overhead tank was opened at exactly the same moment. The simultaneous action of the inlet and waste valves was to remain a basic feature of most valve closets until their manufacture ceased. Cummings's patent also showed that his closet was connected to a water-sealed trap, which ensured that sewer gas from the drain did not pass through the closet into the room.

Cummings's closet, however, possessed one fundamental flaw. Sliding under the bottom of the basin, his valve was not cleaned by the action of the flush and so, over time, acquired a coating of encrusted dirt. In 1778, Joseph Bramah (1749–1814) introduced a closet that replaced the slider with a valve, which was held tight against the bottom of the basin by a spring acting on the main operating lever. When the closet was emptied, the valve dropped down inside an iron valve box immediately below the basin. To use Bramah's own words, it was 'thoroughly washed every time the contents of the basin [were] discharged'. Bramah's closet was a commercial success. In January 1790, the architect John Eveleigh advertised the sale in the *Bath Chronicle* of the 'PATENT WATER CLOSETS, which may be fixed in any parlour, bed or dressing room, without the least effluvia'. A surviving bill of 1793 shows that Bramah supplied six of his 'patent apparatus' to

Joseph Bramah (1749–1814).

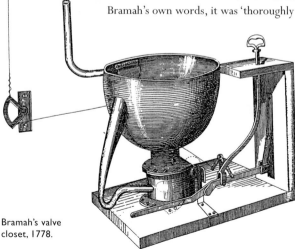

Bramah's valve closet, 1778.

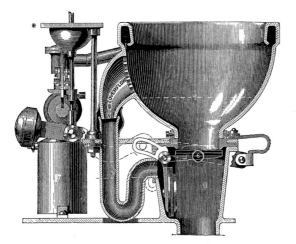

Section of Hellyer's 'Optimus' valve closet with the waste valve open. The cylinder at the bottom left of the diagram is a 'bellows' regulator, first patented by Frederick Underhay in 1852, which ensured that clean flush water filled the basin after use.

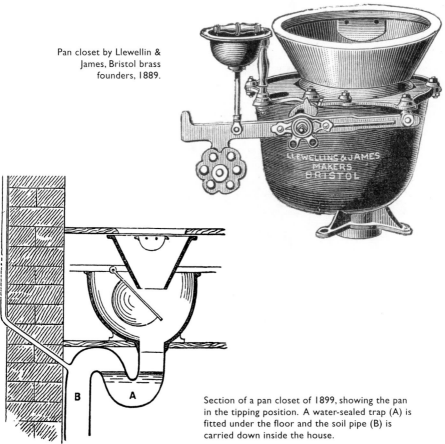

Pan closet by Llewellin & James, Bristol brass founders, 1889.

Section of a pan closet of 1899, showing the pan in the tipping position. A water-sealed trap (A) is fitted under the floor and the soil pipe (B) is carried down inside the house.

Thomas Anson of Shugborough Hall, Staffordshire. By 1797 he claimed to have sold 6,000 water closets.

By the 1820s the 'Bramah' was established as the first-choice WC for the well-to-do. Providing the valve maintained the full level of water in the basin this was an extremely effective closet. The generous quantity of water in the basin helped keep it clean and acted as a secondary seal above the water-sealed trap. They were also virtually silent in operation. With minor modifications they were made throughout the nineteenth century by a large number of sanitary ware manufacturers. As late as the mid 1920s, valve closets were chosen by Edwin Lutyens (1869–1944) for the bathrooms at Castle Drogo in Devon; and Thomas Crapper & Co. continued to make them for special customers until the 1950s.

But valves could be temperamental. A faulty valve – either through loss of seal around the valve seating or a degree of slack in the crank and lever mechanism – would cause the water level in the basin to drop or disappear altogether. The pan closet, which appeared in the late eighteenth century, provided a remedy. Instead of a valve, the water was held in the basin by a copper pan that fitted around the lower part of the basin. The pan was counterbalanced and connected to a lever and crank that tipped the pan down when the closet was flushed. The pan rotated inside a large cast-iron container called a receiver and from there the effluent passed through a trap into the soil pipe. Pan closets first appear in a patent of 1796 taken out by William Law, a London iron founder, and were made throughout the nineteenth century. They were cheaper and more robust than valve closets as the pan always ensured that there was clean water in the basin. In 1857, J. H. Walsh, reviewing the strengths and weaknesses of the various kinds of water closet available in his *Manual of Domestic Economy*, said, 'nothing ... in my opinion comes up to the construction which has been so many years in use and is called the pan closet.'

Superficially, valve and pan closets looked quite similar. The mechanics were hidden from view inside a wooden enclosure – usually of French-

Blue and white earthenware basin for a pan closet basin with a copper fan spreader.

Trade card of Emerson & Howell, Bristol brass founders from 1819 to 1831, showing a pan closet and overhead supply tank filled by the pump seen on the right.

polished mahogany – which supported the fixed seat and lid. The trap, if there was one, was usually under the floorboards and the overhead tank located in a loft space. Assuming the closet was clean, users could admire the interior of the basin, most likely an attractive piece of Staffordshire underglaze printed earthenware, decorated perhaps with an Italian-style landscape of billowing clouds, trees and temples. They might also notice, perhaps, a semi-circular piece of dull copper obscuring part of the design at the rear of the bowl. This was the fan or flushing spreader that fanned out the water across the inside of the basin. Bramah showed one in his patent specification of 1778.

The flush handle was usually nicely made, of cut glass, china or ebony, and set in a brass cup recessed in the seat. Through a system of chains or cables and a lever, a simple weighted valve in the overhead tank was lifted and the flush water tumbled down. As the action was direct and manual, the duration of the pull on the handle governed the length of the flush. There were two obvious drawbacks to this: too short a pull and insufficient water would pass through the closet but too long a pull and the tank could empty. Both valve and pan closets were well established in large houses before the coming of the water carriage system. Few, therefore, were connected to mains water, so the cistern usually had to be filled manually by pumping water up from a basement tank – usually containing rainwater collected off the roof. This arrangement was known by the early 1700s (Lord Chesterfield had a force pump in his London house in 1733 which pumped water up to the cistern above the first-floor water closet) and it remained common in well-appointed houses until the advent of mains water in the 1850s.

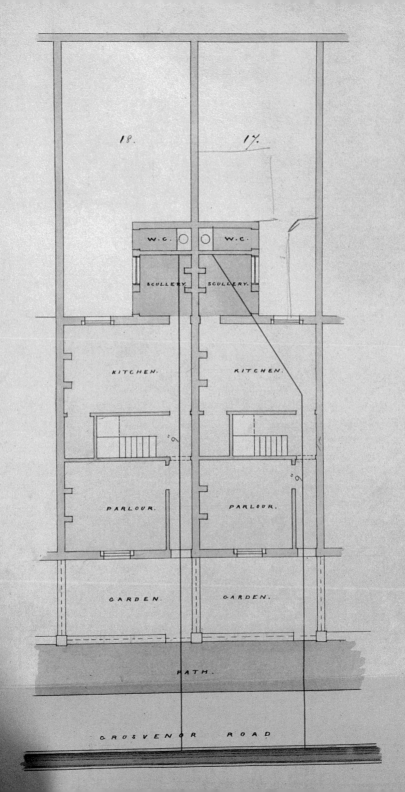

18.

17.

W.C.    W.C.

SCULLERY.    SCULLERY.

KITCHEN.       KITCHEN.

PARLOUR.      PARLOUR.

GARDEN.     GARDEN.

PATH.

GROSVENOR ROAD

# BACK YARD WATER CLOSETS

A Board of Health investigation in London in 1850 found that in the prosperous parish of St James's, Westminster, over 65 per cent of houses had a water closet whilst in Bethnal Green and other poor districts there were but a handful. The water closet was essentially a middle-class, socially exclusive appliance, and was typified by the expensive mechanically operated valve and pan closets, the design of which owed nothing to the considerations of public health. But the spread of water carriage systems in towns from the middle of the century was to lead to the wider use of water closets. After several decades of limited use, the WC was about to be democratised with closets for the masses in their back yards and public lavatories in the street. But sophisticated mechanical closets were considered unsuitable for the poor. In 1873, George Wilson observed, 'In the crowded districts of large towns, the ordinary form of WC has proved a failure partly on account of the complicated character of the contrivances for flushing but chiefly on account of the carelessness and filthy habits of the poorer classes.' Clearly a working-class WC, if it was to work, had to be simple.

So what was considered suitable for the working classes? The answer was a closet without an outlet valve, consisting of an earthenware basin connected directly to a water-sealed trap. There were several different shapes of basin. One was the long hopper: deep and straight-sided with a circular top. This funnel-like shape is featured in a Wedgwood pattern book as early as 1802 and in 1833 J. C. Loudon (1783–1843) illustrated a similar closet in his book *Cottage, Farm & Villa Architecture*. This 'cheap basin and trap' was, he said, 'manufactured at the common tile potteries about London and sold by retail at 2s 6d'. Short hoppers were just like long hoppers, except shorter. Then there were 'cottage' or 'servants'' closet basins, which were like short hoppers, but had sides that were rounded rather than straight and had a slightly oval top. These simple closets, devoid of any mechanics under the seat, were used extensively for working-class housing in towns that had

Opposite:
Plans of working-class terraced houses in Grosvenor Road, Bristol, showing the WCs in the back yard connected to the street sewer, 1859.

Above left:
Hopper basin with
blue and white
transfer
decoration to the
interior.

Above right:
A cottage basin in
cane and white
ware from a house
in Clevedon,
North Somerset.

invested in water carriage systems. They were also installed in the service areas of large houses for servants' use, underlining the social divide typical of a large Victorian house: valve closets, costing upwards of £2 or £3 for the family and simple basin and trap closets costing as little as 3s. for the servants. In the nineteenth century, the closet you sat on defined who you were.

At first glance, a servants' or cottage closet looks remarkably like a modern toilet but there are some important differences. The basin and trap closet was not free standing like most toilets today, but required the support of a wooden enclosure or a plinth of rubble or brickwork with a fixed seat, just like the old privy. The reserve of clean water was held in the trap but, unlike a modern appliance, the trap was fitted immediately below the basin so the water level did not reach the interior of the basin. Without water, excrement tended to stick to the sides of the closet interior. Contemporary opinion was divided on their merits. J. H. Walsh noted that dirt was liable to accumulate in the trap unless the closets were thoroughly flushed and said that in general they were too smelly to be used indoors. But in 1876, a Glasgow sanitary engineer, William Buchan, wrote that his family had used a cottage closet for fifteen years and that the basin was always kept clean by ensuring enough water ran through the closet.

Cottage basin and
trap by Sharpe
Brothers,
Swadlincote,
Derbyshire, fitted
with the company's
patent flushing rim,
1895.

A cottage closet set in brickwork with a fixed wooden seat in the back yard of 9 Rosebery Terrace, Clifton, Bristol, built c.1893–4. Used daily until August 2000, it was removed in March 2001.

An adequate supply of water, therefore, was vital but was often absent. In many working-class homes a basin and trap closet could only be flushed by throwing a bucket of water into the basin, although this often resulted in soaking the fixed wooden seat, or the inadvertent emptying of the trap through syphonic action. A prominent maker of basin and trap closets in the mid nineteenth century was Edmund Sharpe, a sanitary ware potter in Swadlincote, south Derbyshire. In 1855 he took out a patent for a flushing rim. By curling over the rim of the bowl the incoming flush water was carried around the entire rim to wash the interior more effectively than was ever possible with the traditional fan spreader. It was the first patent to specify this important feature that was to become standard on all later closet bowls, but

The 'Bristol
Closet' by W. H. &
T. B. Cottrell,
registered in 1884.

as so often with patents, it did not record the original idea: Sharpe's patent
merely described an improved hollow flushing rim.

By the 1870s, most basin and trap closets were fitted with a hollow rim
and a spigot at the rear to provide an end-on connection to the flush pipe.
Even so, as late as 1884, Messrs. W. H. & T. B. Cottrell of Bristol registered a
design for the 'Bristol Closet', which had no flushing rim. An example survives
in Bristol Museum and Art Gallery: a deep, round-topped basin – crude and
heavy – resembling the bowl of a giant clay tobacco pipe and made of purple-
brown stoneware. Arrangements for providing flush water for hopper closets
were often idiosyncratic and insanitary, as Francis Vacher, the Medical Officer
for Birkenhead and District, reported in 1889. Many, he found, were flushed
by an ordinary mains tap placed near the rim but this trickling spiral of water
lacked sufficient force to scour out the interior. And if the trap became choked,
filling the basin, there was always the risk that foul water could be drawn into
the tap and contaminate public supplies. One he found was flushed with the
dirty, greasy water from the kitchen sink and, as the connection between the
two was not trapped, foul air from the closet could return to the sink. It was,

he said, 'horribly disgusting'. But surely the worst arrangement he saw was a hopper basin simply planted in the ground: apparently it was called, somewhat quaintly, a 'dry water closet'! Nevertheless, it was the poor image of hopper closets, not their poor performance, which ultimately circumscribed their use: this was a WC associated with artisans and mechanics, servants and cottage dwellers – not ladies and gentlemen.

Further down the social scale, for the 'rougher class of labourers and the like', an even simpler arrangement had appeared by the mid 1850s. This was the trough closet, a communal arrangement usually accommodated in a separate block, which consisted of a bench containing two or more holes, each divided by a partition above the seat. The closet discharged into a trough containing water, which was emptied either manually through pulling a plug or automatically. These were widely used on Merseyside and in institutions 'where ordinary arrangements for flushing would be likely to be misused or altogether neglected'. The trough, or 'water closet range', won the general approval of sanitarians in the second half of the nineteenth century, yet this was a far from satisfactory installation. Unlike most other types of water closet, the waste of a trough closet was not carried away instantly but was left decomposing under the seat, causing a stench and providing a likely means of spreading contagious diseases. They were eventually condemned as insanitary and were phased out in Liverpool and doubtless elsewhere in the early 1900s. Improved trough closets with separate traps and automatic flushes, however, continued to be made long afterwards.

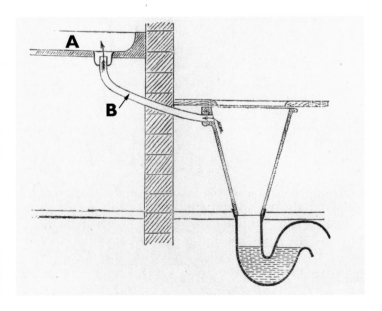

A sanitary horror of 1889. A hopper closet is flushed with dirty, greasy slop water from a stone sink (A), while foul air from the closet returns to the sink through the untrapped waste pipe (B).

THE
"DELUGE."

# THE RISE OF THE
# PEDESTAL WATER CLOSET

THE development of the WC in the middle of the nineteenth century had reached a stage where a limited range of closets was in production, sharply divided by social class, quality and efficiency. Following Bramah's patent of 1778, no sanitary engineering genius had appeared to take the development of the water closet forward. Between 1800 and 1850, just twenty-three patents were taken out for water closets. Most were for minor improvements to existing types, such as William Downe's patent of 1825 for a smaller container for pan closets. Then, in 1851, a new name came to prominence: Josiah George Jennings (1810–82), arguably the greatest sanitary engineer of the nineteenth century. Based in Southwark, London, Jennings persuaded the Commission organising the Great Exhibition to install public toilets in the Crystal Palace. 'The subject is a peculiar one, and very difficult to handle', he wrote, 'but no false delicacy ought to prevent immediate attention being given to matters affecting the health and comfort of the thousands who throng the thoroughfares of your city.' Jennings's facilities at the Great Exhibition were an enormous success and over 827,000 visitors paid a penny to use them; it was from this time that a new piece of sanitary parlance entered the English language: 'spending a penny'. Jennings also provided urinals for men but their use was free.

For the first-class refreshment rooms he installed expensive mechanical valve closets of his own design but for the second-class facilities he devised an entirely new type of WC. This was essentially a modified basin and trap closet. There were no valves, just a simple all-earthenware appliance with a water-sealed trap below a basin containing a shallow pool of water to drown solids. Jennings patented this closet the following year although he subsequently claimed to have designed it before the exhibition. He called it the 'Monkey' closet – perhaps implying that it was simple enough for a monkey to use – but it was by another name, the 'wash-out' closet, that it was to enjoy considerable success from the mid 1870s.

The 'Deluge' pedestal wash-down closet by Twyford with raised decoration and original toilet paper holder behind the seat.

THE POUND AND THE SHILLING.
"Whoever Thought of Meeting You Here!"

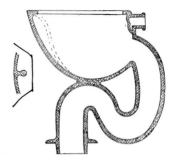

Left:
The Great Exhibition, 1851.
The working classes, left,
could visit the exhibition
for a shilling but their
second-class refreshment
rooms contained Jennings's
simple 'Monkey' closet. The
first-class facilities for the
well-to-do were equipped
with more expensive valve
closets. From Punch, 1851.

Above:
George Jennings's
'Monkey' closet
patented in 1852
following its use at
the Great
Exhibition the
previous year.

Below left:
Pillar type urinal, the
'Adamant' by Twyford,
1900.

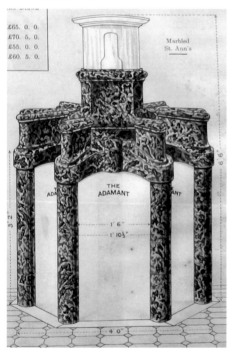

£65. 0. 0.
£70. 5. 0.
£55. 0. 0.
£60. 5. 0.

Marbled
St. Ann's

THE
ADAMANT

Jennings was a pioneer of public conveniences, which were established in London from the 1850s: he is credited with the idea of placing urinals in a circle around a central pillar. In 1858 he took out his first patent for another new type of water closet, the twin basin or 'plug' closet. In these the waste was discharged by depressing a plunger or piston housed in a 'plug chamber' or cylinder to the rear or side of the basin. When the plug was raised, the flush water was released at the same time, washing the contents of the basin through a connection to the rear chamber and then through the trap. There were few metal parts and the plug cylinder, basin and trap were

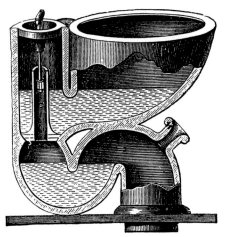
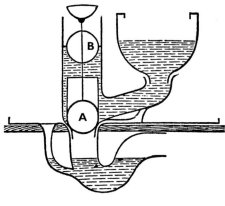

made of one piece of earthenware. They were widely commended for their simplicity and enjoyed considerable success. In 1863, John Shanks (1825–95), then a little-known plumber in Barrhead near Glasgow, introduced his own version, which had an india-rubber ball for a plug. It was largely on this, his 'Patent Flexible Valve Closet' (or 'Number Four' as it was known in the works), that his early success was established. Similar closets also enjoyed widespread success in America. A closet with a plunger was granted a United States patent as early as 1857 and by the early 1880s J. L. Mott of New York and Chicago was offering three models with plunger wastes patented by John Demarest: the 'Demarest', the 'Hygeia' and the 'Premier'.

Jennings, Shanks and others were beginning to take water closet technology in new directions but it was only after 1870 that the pace of development quickened. There then followed an extraordinary period of frenzied activity, lasting little more than fifteen years, when the water closet was changed beyond all recognition and the shape of the WC – or toilet – familiar to us all today was established. Perhaps it was the impact of the Prince of Wales's near-death in late 1871 (attributed, as we have seen, to defective sanitary arrangements) that stimulated public interest in sanitary science. After all, if the Prince could be a plumber, why should Jennings and others worry about public reaction to this 'peculiar' and 'difficult' subject?

After 1870, the volume of literature on the subject increased. An early publication was William Eassie's 1872 book *Healthy Houses,* and in 1877 Samuel Stephens Hellyer wrote his highly influential book *The Plumber and Sanitary House,* which eventually ran to six editions and was even translated

Above left:
George Jennings's plug closet, introduced in 1858.

Above right:
Shanks's 'Number 4' plug closet introduced in 1863. 'A' is the plug and 'B' the ballcock regulating the water supply to the cistern.

43

Above:
First edition of
*The Plumber and
Sanitary Houses*,
by Samuel
Stephens Hellyer,

into French. Suddenly sanitary science was topical. Through these and other publications the relative merits of the various types of water closet were, for the first time, brought before a wider readership. In 1877, the Sanitary Institute was founded and at its annual trade shows (the first one was at Stafford the following year) water closets were subject to rigorous testing to assess their effectiveness. Two closets were quickly exposed as insanitary. The first – hardly surprisingly – was the long hopper: Hellyer said that rather than being used as closets the earthenware funnels would better serve as rhubarb forcers! If the shortcomings of the long hopper were all too visible, the exposure of the pan closet as a danger to health was probably, for some, more of a surprise, but the shortcomings of this popular closet were hidden from view. The problem was the interior of the receiver: it was simply impossible for flush water to scour clean the underside of the pan. Hellyer reckoned that, on average, a pan could accrue 2 pounds of dried excrement; the only effective way of cleaning one was to detach it and burn off the dirt in the kitchen fire.

The shortcomings of the pan closet were usually compounded by the use of the 'D trap', made of sheet lead, which was not self-cleansing and harboured dirty water, releasing a bad smell every time the appliance was

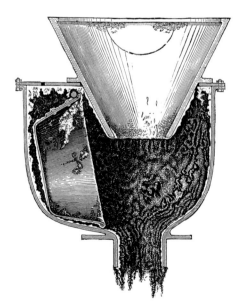

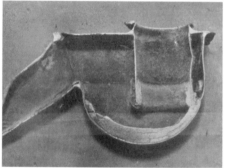

Left:
Hellyer's pan closet in action showing graphically how waste matter swirled around the interior and stuck to the sides.

Above:
An old lead D trap that was removed from a house in July 1899, shown sectioned in the sixth edition of Hellyer's book to show how filth could accumulate in the nooks and corners of its large interior.

used. 'The puffs of bad smells, which such apparatus send up, after they have been fixed for some time, are enough to make one wish for the old fashioned privy again', wrote Hellyer in 1877. Two years later, Eassie said, 'I would like to see abolished the filthy D trap with its furrings of faecal matter, the huge iron container with its linings of ancient ordure and the trap at the foot of the soil pipe with its excremental cesspit.' By 1879, the days of the pan closet were well and truly numbered.

Another early casualty was the twin basin or plunger closet. Some had been made without a water-sealed trap and these came in for particular disapprobation. Moreover, the plug and its chamber, it was found over time, could become 'dirty and insanitary'. From the mid 1870s, it was Jennings's 'Monkey' basin and trap closet, introduced some twenty-five years earlier, that was attracting all the attention and winning the plaudits. From 1875, several manufacturers took out patents for improvements to this arrangement of basin and trap. The first was a Swadlincote potter, Samuel Hunt Rowley, who seems to have stolen the idea from Hellyer in London after receiving an order to manufacture some to Hellyer's design. It was Rowley's partner, James Woodward, incidentally, who in 1878 registered the name 'wash-out', which was soon universally recognised for closets of this type. Hellyer quickly responded with a new design – this time protected by patent – and in 1877, a Brighton plumber, Daniel Bostel, introduced the 'Brighton Excelsior'. Doulton launched the 'Lambeth' while in Hanley, Stoke-on-Trent, the 'National' made its debut in Thomas Twyford's range of sanitary ware in March 1879.

The 'Brighton Excelsior' wash-out closet introduced by Daniel Bostel in 1877. The closet has a double supply and an inspection cover over the trap.

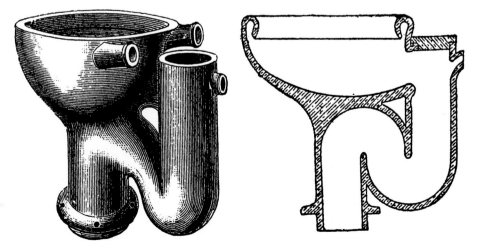

Doulton's
'Lambeth' wash-
out closet with
exposed trap
finished with
raised ornament.

There had been Twyfords involved in potting in north Staffordshire since the seventeenth century. Thomas Twyford (1826–72) turned almost exclusively to the manufacture of sanitary ware in Hanley in 1849, but it was under his son, Thomas William Twyford (1849–1921), that the company established itself from the 1870s as one of Britain's leading sanitary ware

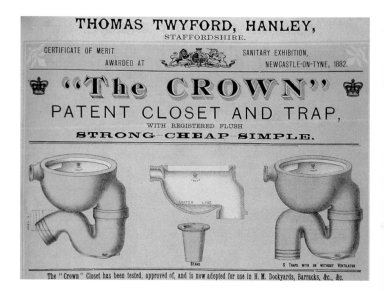

The 'Crown' basin
and trap closet
with wash-out
arrangement by
Twyford, 1883.

manufacturers. Increasingly, the development of the WC was in the hands of sanitary potters like Twyford and Doulton. Jennings had established a pottery near Poole in 1854 and Shanks followed with the Victoria Pottery at Barrhead for the manufacture of fireclay sanitary ware in 1902.

By 1880, the future seemed to lie with the wash-out closet. From second-class public WC to a fully domestic appliance, the rising popularity of the wash-out closet from the mid 1870s coincided with the rapid adoption of the bathroom in middle-class homes. Before 1870, few houses were built with bathrooms but in the 1870s the first-floor plan of the typical large villa was redesigned to accommodate a bathroom containing a fixed bath, lavatory wash basin and WC. Unlike most other basin and trap closets, the suitability of the wash-out for this new room in the house was beyond all doubt. However, wash-out closets of the late 1870s were not free standing and they required the support of a wooden enclosure which was finished *en suite* with the bath and washbasin. But in this time of rapid change it was not long before enclosed fittings were condemned as insanitary for harbouring dirt and germs. By the early 1880s, advanced sanitary theory was promoting the idea of free-standing sanitary appliances that could easily be kept clean and safe.

Thomas William Twyford (1849–1921).

Some of the earliest free-standing closets, such as Doulton's 'Combination' and Twyford's first examples of the 'Unitas', retained an exposed trap below the basin and still looked rather awkward. A. Dimmock & Co. of Hanley ingeniously disguised the trap of their 'Dolphin' wash-out closet, introduced at the end of 1884, as the body of a sea serpent holding a giant sea shell – the basin – in its jaws. But earlier the same year, in May, at the International Health Exhibition held in South Kensington, George Jennings & Co. launched the 'Pedestal Vase'. This was a wash-out closet in action but for probably the very first time the pedestal supporting the closet also contained the trap. This sleek appliance was completely free standing and made in one piece of earthenware: in its modelling and firing this was a spectacular demonstration of the artistry and skill of the sanitary potter.

The potter released the WC from its wooden enclosure, and transformed it into a piece of ceramic art. Twyford soon remodelled the 'Unitas', with its oak leaf and acorn relief decoration, as a fully enclosed pedestal closet; and a second styling, 'Florentine', followed in 1886. Doulton's 'Combination' re-appeared as a sinuous all-in-one closet with the trap enclosed inside the skirting; Shanks's answer was their 'Tubal' pedestal wash-out. Three further highly ornate pedestal closets appeared in 1886: Baxendale of Manchester

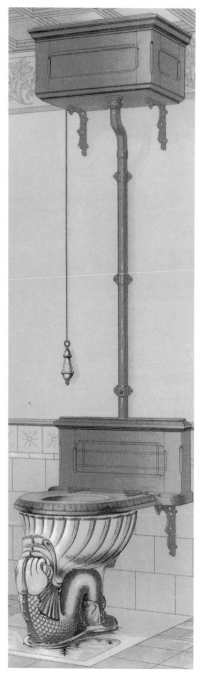

Left:
The 'Dolphin' wash-out closet by Dimmock & Co. of Hanley, Stoke-on-Trent, featured in the catalogue of J. L. Mott, New York, 1888.

Above:
The 'Pedestal Vase' by George Jennings, introduced in 1884.

Below:
George Jennings's manufacturer's mark from a surviving 'Pedestal Vase', c.1885.

Above:
The 'Pedestal Vase' wash-out closet with enclosed trap by George Jennings, 1884.

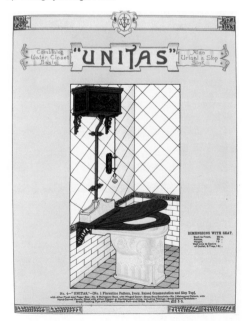

Above:
The 'Nautilus', a one-piece pedestal closet introduced in 1886 by Smeaton & Co., London.

Left:
Twyford's 'Unitas' wash-out closet with raised ornament in the 'Florentine' style, 1887.

49

chose a recumbent lion to support the basin while the London firm Smeaton & Co. introduced the 'Amphora' and 'Nautilus'.

The pedestal WC was usually fitted with a lifting seat fixed not to the basin but to ornate cast-iron wall brackets. This enabled the closet to be used as a urinal by men and a slop sink for the disposal of waste from chamber pots, without, as Twyford claimed in 1888, 'the wetting so objectionable in closets having permanent seats'. But not everyone was convinced. In 1881, Hellyer wrote, 'as it has now become the bad practice with many men to treat such closets as if they were urinals, it will generally be found that there is more filth outside such closets than inside.' On this debate, perhaps, we should allow Twyford the final say with these words from an 1888

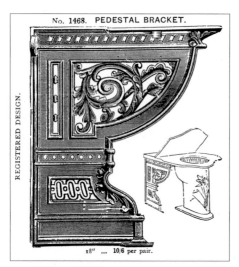

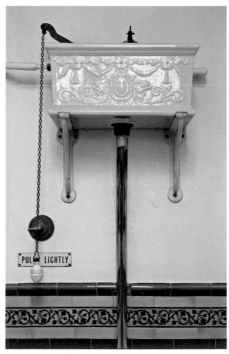

Above left:
Ornate cast-iron bracket for lifting closet seat, c.1895.

Left:
The 'Paisley' syphon water waste preventer in cast iron made by Doulton at their Paisley iron foundry established in 1888.

Above right:
Ceramic casing, chain and pull handle for an overhead WWP by Twyford, c.1890.

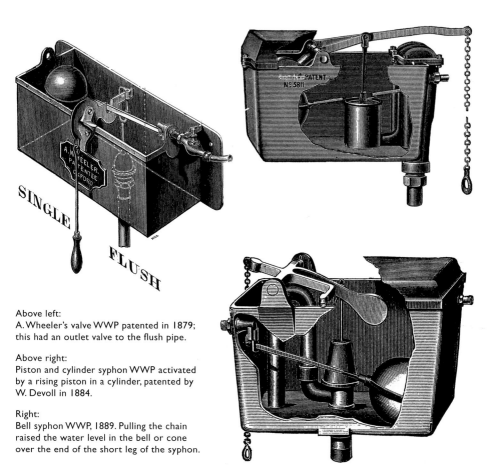

Above left:
A. Wheeler's valve WWP patented in 1879; this had an outlet valve to the flush pipe.

Above right:
Piston and cylinder syphon WWP activated by a rising piston in a cylinder, patented by W. Devoll in 1884.

Right:
Bell syphon WWP, 1889. Pulling the chain raised the water level in the bell or cone over the end of the short leg of the syphon.

advertisement: 'Unlike ordinary WC basins … neither filth, nor anything causing offensive smells can accumulate … free access can be had to all parts of the basin and trap so that everything about the closet can be kept clean.'

Pedestal closets were usually connected to a small overhead cistern with a chain pull and containing just enough water for a single flush. To the Victorian sanitary engineer and plumber, this was the 'water waste preventer' or 'WWP'. They first appeared in the 1850s and were subject to hundreds of patents in the second half of the nineteenth century to ensure that the supply to the cistern, governed by a ballcock, was closed when the cistern was in operation. Many relied on valves to release their charge of water but valves can leak, causing waste. From the 1870s, regulations issued by local water authorities encouraged the use of syphonic cisterns operating on a 'pull and let go' principle. Upon pulling the chain, a simple mechanism raised the level of water inside the tank and over the top of a syphon pipe. Once charged, the syphonic action continued – independently of any further tugging of the chain – until it was emptied. George Jennings was the first to patent one in 1854 using the principle of water displacement to raise the water over the down pipe, but from the 1870s, syphons charged by raising a cast-iron 'bell' or a piston inside a cylinder became almost universal. They could not leak, there were few working parts to go wrong and many survive in use, especially in public toilets today.

From the 1870s, most water authorities set the maximum capacity of cisterns at 2 gallons. For Hellyer this limit was absurdly low; nevertheless, in this critical period of development, the 2-gallon limit was clearly an important factor in determining the success or failure of a particular type of closet. It was quite likely that no quantity of water was ever going to clean out the receiver of a pan closet, but 2 gallons was wholly inadequate. It was yet another blow for the type. Wash-out closets, at first, fared better. In an official test at the International Health Exhibition, Jennings's 'Pedestal Vase' was coupled to a 2-gallon syphonic cistern and successfully disposed of ten apples, a flat sponge and four pieces of sanitary paper stuck to the sides with plumbers' smudge: it was awarded a gold medal. But doubts about the effectiveness of wash-out closets began to surface. The depth of water in the basin was often insufficient to cover the faeces deposited, causing a stench, especially when, as Hellyer pointed out, a 'long seat holder' was in occupation. It was also found that by the time the flush had cleared the basin it had insufficient force to clear out the trap.

Hellyer's original two-piece 'Artisan' of the 1870s (left), and a later one-piece pedestal example with relief decoration, 1899 (right).

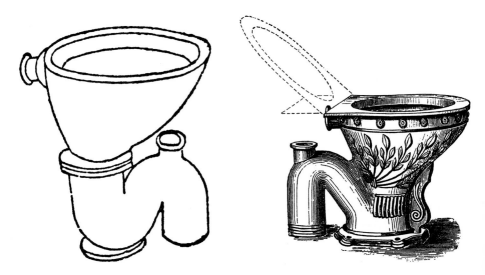

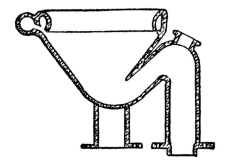
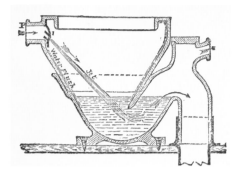

From the mid 1880s, support grew for a new type of basin and trap water closet: the wash-down. It was developed from the short hopper or cottage basin and was, indeed, very similar but with one critical difference: the trap was set higher so that it effectively became a continuation of the basin. So now, the water level – instead of being confined to a trap fitted below the basin, leaving it dry – was now shared between the trap and basin. The higher water level in the basin reduced the exposed surface liable to be fouled. As Hellyer clearly explained in 1891, 'the force of the flush, instead of spending itself upon the basin as in the wash-out, passes through the trap with a scouring action washing the whole of the interior'. It was a small improvement to a well-known, if little-regarded, type of closet, but it was a crucial development and was to spell the end of the short-lived supremacy of the wash-out closet in Britain.

The effectiveness of the wash-down was beyond all doubt. Percy Boulnois stated that it was 'probably the best for all purposes that can be had'. This was to become the toilet of everyday use in the twentieth century, familiar across the world. It was a British invention with an impact on standards of domestic comfort, personal hygiene and public health that can hardly be overstated, but whose invention was it? Strangely, we may never know for sure. The wash-down made an inauspicious start at about the same time that interest in the wash-out was increasing. At least three sanitary ware manufacturers launched versions in the late 1870s. The first was Hellyer. In 1877 he introduced a basin and trap closet with a small oval basin although the trap was still clearly below the basin: he called it the 'Artisan'. The following year, however, he patented a one-piece closet, the 'Vortex', which brought the basin and trap so close together that the bottom of the basin also served as the bottom of the trap. This WC, Hellyer later claimed, provided a larger exposed surface of water than any previous basin and trap closet. Then, in March 1879, Twyford launched a new catalogue of earthenware sanitary

Above left: Hellyer's 'Vortex' closet patented in Britain in 1878 and in the USA in 1880.

Above right: Buchan's 'Carmichael' closet introduced in 1879. In the 1892 edition of his textbook on plumbing Buchan laid claim to the invention of the 'wash-down'. The name – if not the concept – may well have indeed been his.

In 1879 Twyford's 'Lillyman's' closet pointed the way to the future, but in the firm's catalogue of March that year it shared a page with basins for closets of the very worst kind – pans, hoppers and servants' basins.

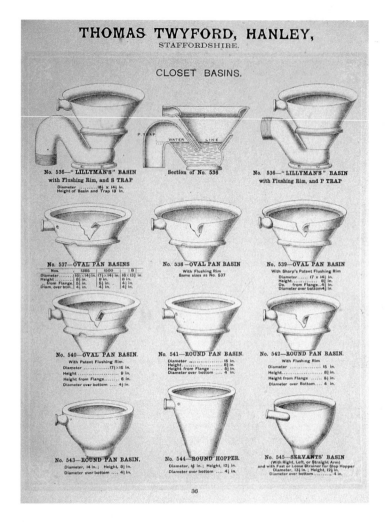

goods that featured the 'Lillyman', which clearly brought the water-sealed trap into the basin. Later that year, in December, William Buchan, who as we know had already used a cottage basin with success, took out a patent for a similar closet: the 'Carmichael'. This model almost certainly took its name from Dr Neil Carmichael, a Glasgow doctor who spoke strongly in favour of basin and trap closets on the wash-down arrangement at a meeting of the Glasgow Philosophical Society in February 1880.

But none of these makers can be given the credit for the original idea. As early as the 1850s and 1860s, several British patents were taken out for basin and trap closets with the trap set high enough to provide water in the basin. Indeed, Hellyer said little about the 'Artisan' in the first edition of his book in 1877, except that it was cheap. Only gradually, it appears, did he come to appreciate its full potential. Writing about the 'Artisan' in January 1886, he announced, 'as the closet is fixed … largely for general purposes as for the use of mechanics and domestics and exception having been taken to the name 'Artisan', it has been renamed the 'Hygienic'.' He not only changed the name but also raised the water level in line with the 'Vortex' by bringing the trap closer to the basin.

Support for this type of closet was growing, albeit slowly, in France and Belgium and also across the Atlantic. In 1884 Glenn Brown, an architect from Washington DC, wrote of the 'cleanliness, simplicity and effectiveness' of basin and trap closets of this kind. He still referred to them as 'short hoppers' but the term 'wash-down' soon became general and may well have been coined by William Buchan in Glasgow: he had attached it to his 'Carmichael' closet by 1884. The following year, a London sanitary engineer and former apprentice of Thomas Crapper named Frederick Humpherson (1854–1919) took its development a stage further by producing the first pedestal version, the 'Beaufort', named after his works in Chelsea. It was made in one piece with the trap neatly enclosed in the plinth. He called it a 'flush-down' and it made its debut at the 1885 meeting of the Sanitary Institute in Leicester. Here was the first modern pedestal wash-down – the WC of the future – and although the verdict was favourable (it was awarded a Certificate of Merit),

Below left: Frederick Humpherson (1854–1919).

Below right: The 'Beaufort' pedestal wash-down closet by Frederick Humpherson in cane and white ware.

Above left:
The 'Improved Marlborough' pedestal wash-down closet by Thomas Crapper, c.1895.

Above right:
The 'Invictas' pedestal wash-down closet by Johnson Brothers, 1891.

the response was somewhat muted: it was actually eclipsed by two dry privies on show, which both came away with higher awards!

But other manufacturers were clearly keeping a close eye on developments. In 1887 Twyford introduced the 'Deluge' wash-down as a cheap two-piece basin and trap closet but in 1889 it was remodelled as a handsome, one-piece ceramic WC with the trap fully enclosed within the pedestal base. By about 1890, most other makers had added a pedestal wash-down to their range. Doulton had their appropriately named 'Simplicitas'; Shanks, the 'Citizen'; and Thomas Crapper, the 'Marlborough'. There were many other models supplied by leading firms, including Dent & Hellyer, George Jennings, J. Tylor & Sons, Johnson Brothers, Sharpe Brothers and Morrison, Ingram & Co. Like the wash-out WCs a few years earlier, they were available in a wide range of finishes ranging from 'cane and white' fireclay at the bottom end of the market to highly ornate models complete with decoration in relief, colour, or a combination of both. Designs printed in one underglaze colour, usually blue or brown, were popular. Then there were the more expensive polychrome patterns, often consisting of Japanese-inspired floral designs, which combined hand painting with underglaze printing. In the 1890s, Twyford's two 'top of the range' finishes were the magnificent 'Venetian' pattern of raised ornament in cobalt blue and gold and the 'Corinthian', which used coloured slips, applied like cake icing, to create raised ornament; Twyford called it *'Pâte Dure'*.

But the success of the wash-down did not bring to a close this period of feverish experiment and innovation. Sanitary engineers, it seems, still felt a duty to provide simple closets for simple folk – for people incapable, it was believed, of pulling a flush. So the provision of automatic closets continued and in 1887 James Duckett, a brick and tile maker in Burnley, east Lancashire, brought out his 'Automatic Slop Water Closet'. Universally known as the tipper closet or 'tippler', they were also intended for use in towns where water was in short supply. These were back yard closets and automatically flushed by a 3-gallon stoneware tipping tank fed from the kitchen sink or from rain and surface water. When the tank was almost full, it tipped over, sending a powerful flush along a drain pipe to the water-sealed trap at the base of the closet.

So the responsibility for flushing the device was taken out of the hands of the user and it is well recorded that many a quiet and private moment on this type of closet was rudely interrupted by the wholly unexpected crash and tumble of the tipper releasing its flush. These closets with their distinctive purple-brown stoneware pedestals were widely used in working-class housing in the Pennine towns of Lancashire and Yorkshire from the 1890s. But from their debut at the 1887 Sanitary Exhibition in Bolton, there were reservations about their performance. The flush water passed through the trap but not the pedestal, so there was no provision for removing excrement stuck to its sides. And they required regular tipping of that tank: if not, they could become very dirty and smelly.

As a back yard closet, the adoption of the tipper was strictly limited to working-class housing but in the 1890s a new type of WC appeared that, at the time, some believed might even replace the wash-down. This was the

By the 1890s even the traditional valve closet was available in pedestal form. This is Hellyer's 'Optimus' valve closet enclosed in a free-standing pedestal, 1899.

The 'Twycliffe' syphonic WC with pedestal and matching overhead cistern in the 'Venetian' pattern, 1894.

syphonic closet which used a syphon to draw out the waste instead of relying on the power of the flush to force it out. An American, John Randall Mann, had taken out a British patent for a closet with syphonic action in 1870. Further patents followed but it was only in 1894, when, in quick succession, Shanks, Jennings and Twyford introduced syphonic closets, that the type began to attract serious attention. Jennings's model was the 'Closet of the Century', and used two traps to trigger the syphon: by directing the flush to the lower trap, air displacement pulled the basin's contents from the one above. But the styling of the 'Closet of the Century' was rather dated. In order to hide the ugly pipe work at the back, the device was enclosed in wood complete with a traditional pull handle recessed in the seat to operate the flush. However, in the 'Twycliffe' syphonic closet, Twyford created a thoroughly modern one-piece pedestal WC that incorporated two integral flushing pipes: these directed jets of water to the basin and behind the trap to charge the syphon. The syphonic closet was practically silent in operation and, as the discharge of the waste was not dependent upon the force of the flush, it was possible to provide a greater depth of water in the basin. But the design had its own particular problems: the jet orifice on a 'Twycliffe', for example, could clog with dirt and it was expensive. So it was the wash-down – simple, reliable, and (importantly) cheap and affordable – that went forward to become the universal toilet of the twentieth century.

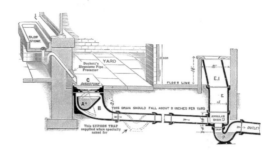

Section of a tipper closet from the 1914 catalogue of Duckett & Sons, Burnley.

Duckett's slop water tipper closet in stoneware with fluted pedestal and tipper tank below ground level at the rear.

# THE WATER CLOSET
# AFTER 1900

COMPARED to the period 1851–1900, the development of the WC in the twentieth century was less dramatic. In the early 1900s, the name 'toilet' caught on and the exuberance of the colour and relief ornament of the late-Victorian pedestal WC was suppressed under a wave of sanitary puritanism. Decoration was condemned as insanitary. It interfered with function – it could harbour dirt and germs – so it had to go. By 1910, the only approved colour for bathroom appliances was white, and without ornament the toilet suddenly became rather dull. Even the arrival of art deco from the mid 1920s – jazzy, geometric and challenging – resulted in nothing more exciting than the idea of the 'cut corner', the angled treatment to the base of the pedestal. The 1930s, at least, saw the return of colour and the use of bakelite for the seats. Coloured sanitary ware had first appeared in the United States in 1927. It created quite a stir and by 1929 had reached Britain. By the early 1930s, every hardware catalogue was illustrated with bathroom suites in a range of mainly blues, greens and yellows, although for the bold and brave they could be had in black. Bakelite was introduced for the seats and lids in a limited range of colours. One of these was black and if the black toilet seat began life at the cutting edge of 'jazz style' around 1930, it soon became the dreariest of choices, widely used for public toilets everywhere.

The 1930s also saw the widespread adoption of close-coupled and low-level cisterns. Shanks had introduced these as early as 1893, when they were made of cast iron. But the 1930s cistern was made of earthenware and matched the basin in style and colour. In the 1950s, the traditional materials of the WC (earthenware and fireclay) were replaced by 'vitreous china', a dense, non-porous pottery that was also used in America. In the late 1960s and 1970s, new colours appeared including the melancholy 'Avocado' and the muted 'Pampas', although closets in wine red, dark brown and deep blue struck a bolder note. Then the 1990s saw a wholesale rejection of colour with a return to white. There was even a revival of the late-Victorian styles.

Opposite:
A bathroom suite in green with a low level WC with coloured seat and lid, 1932. It was also available in blue, dove grey and amber.

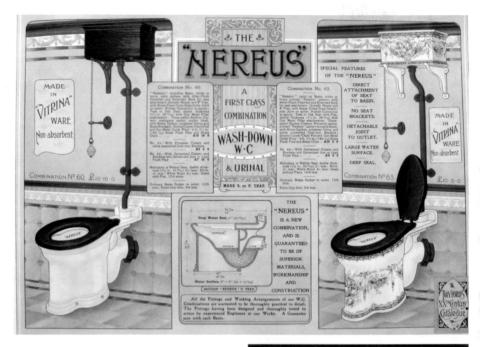

Above: The 'Nereus' wash-down WC from Twyford's 'Twentieth Century Catalogue' of 1900.

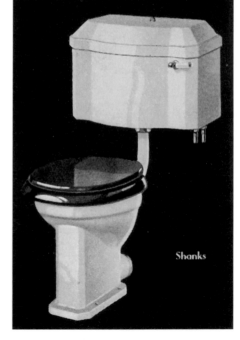

At the same time the industry reworked the outward shape of the toilet to give it a contemporary look, but the toilet most people still use today is essentially the WC created by Victorian sanitary engineers and public health reformers after 1850. As such, the twenty-first century toilet remains essentially their achievement.

Shanks's 'Torentia' close-coupled WC in pink, 1936.

# FURTHER READING

Blaire, M. *Ceramic Water Closets*. Shire, 2000.

Celoria, F. *Water Closets, Past Present and Future*. Gladstone Pottery Museum, Stoke-on-Trent, 1981.

Eveleigh, D. J. *Bogs, Baths & Basins*. Sutton, Stroud, 2002.

Gregory, M. E., and James, S. *Toilets of the World*. Merrell, London and New York, 2006.

Hall, L. *Down the Garden Path*. Countryside Books, Newbury, 2001.

Halliday, S. *The Great Stink of London*. Sutton, Stroud, 1999.

Hart Davies. *Thunder, Flush and Thomas Crapper*. Michael O'Mara Books, London, 1997.

Lambton, L. *Temples of Convenience*. Gordon Fraser, London, 1978.

Lambton, L. *Temples of Convenience and Chambers of Delight*. Pavilion, London, 1995.

Palmer. *The Water Closet, A New History*. David & Charles, Newton Abbot, 1973.

Reyburn, W. *Flushed with Pride, The Story of Thomas Crapper*. Macdonald & Co., 1969 and Pavilion 1989.

Sale, C. *The Specialist*. Putnam & Co., London, 1930.

Wedd, K. *The Victorian Bathroom Catalogue*. Studio Editions, 1996.

Wright, L. *Clean and Decent*. Routledge and Kegan Paul, 1960.

Shanks's 'Combination' wash-down pedestal closet with low level cast-iron cistern, 1893.

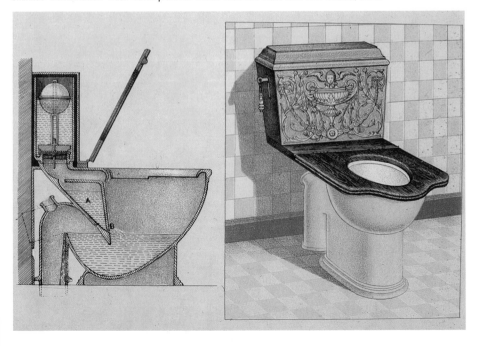

# INDEX

*Page numbers in italic refer to illustrations*